Email Marketing

Machine

By
Leo Thomas

Introduction

Email Marketing Facts –

There are roughly 22,000,000,000 (22 Billion) emails sent EVERY hour.

Average Open Rate – 11% – 15%

Average Click Through Rate – 2.1% – 5%

I can teach you a lot about email marketing! Here's how...

How do you make sure YOUR email gets the attention it deserves? You're about to be amazed as I reveal the tactics that allowed me to build one of the UK's largest niche businesses over the past 14 years.

I have sent millions of 'permission based / double opt-in' emails and generated millions in sales as a result.

This book may not be as long as some books on email marketing.

Please don't judge the book by the length. I just wanted to give you quality information that I know works and is highly effective… **but in a compact format.**

One that is easy to follow and allows you to put into practice all the techniques and strategies you'll discover without all the fluff and padding.

Email marketing is a crucial part of any business and done effectively is highly profitable.

There are a few techniques that you can use now to make every one of your email campaigns far more effective and generate more impressive results.

I've learnt the majority of these techniques the hard way through trial and error. I've been using email marketing since 2000 and built lists into the tens of thousands of subscribers in very, very narrow markets.

The good news for you is it can be done easier today than at anytime before. The software is better and easier to use. There has been more research on what works the best and I want to reveal it all to you so you can develop a highly effective email marketing machine that deliveries the results you want.

Inside this book you'll discover everything you need to know including:

- The best times of day to send email marketing
- The days of the week that will generate the best results (and the days to avoid)
- Subject lines that increase open rates
- Highly effective emails ideas for different types of jobs
- Clever ways to increase the number of targeted subscribers you receive
- Popular and under the radar software that you can use
- What you MUST avoid to ensure your emails are delivered.
- Avoiding Google's promotion filter
- My favourite method of increasing subscribers
- Ways to improve your conversion rate
- Produce better emails using these tactics
- When to use specific types of emails
- What to do straight after someone subscribes (and it's probably not what you think)

And lots, lots more…

The aim of this book is to make you an email marketing master and help you produce results you could have only dreamed of before.

You can make a lot of money using email marketing effectively and here's how…

Plus you can get even more ideas by joining us FREE at

www.EmailMarketingBonus.com

How to Easily Get More Subscribers

First off remember the quality of your subscribers is highly important. Don't aim for a huge list; you want a quality responsive list. The higher your open and click through rate, the better.

I have heard of people making thousands every month by having tiny lists but each reader is highly engaged with the author.

Equally there are owners who have lists of tens of thousands that only make a few sales.

I want to explain to you the difference and show you exactly how you can make each subscriber count and generate money for you. There are a few strategies and techniques that will make all the difference.

But first you have to build yourself a quality list – How?

You want to **aim for quality every time**. A list of buyers is clearly much better than a list of non-buyers; they should be more responsive and open to an offer from you. If your email subscribers love you then there is less chance your email will get marked as spam.

The good news is that it's not hard to build a list (especially if you already have visitors – but if not I'll still show you the methods you can use) by following a few simple steps.

You'll definitely want to read the section below on 'lead magnets' for a detailed method that is really effective in building new subscribers.

For the basis of this book I will assume you have an 'offer or product' or you have a reason you want to collect subscribers. You need to connect with these people and give them a valid reason for subscribing.

You probably already have a good idea who your audience is, but it's always worth checking (and check on your competitors as well).

Have a look at

www.quantcast.com

www.alexa.com/siteinfo

There are a lot of really good quality companies in this space and in all honesty you probably will not find much difference between the main leaders.

The email service provider will provide everything you need to run a successful email marketing campaign and autoresponder series.

They will help you create the sign up box and give you a few different ways you can present it. Some will give you the code to install yourself, others will host it, or you can choose. But most of them are now really easy to use with WYSISWYG (what you see is what you get) technology. They have tried to simplify it so that even the most non-technical person can use it easily.

These providers will help you automate the whole list building process and make it super easy for you and your subscribers. They'll manage unsubscribes, bounced emails and ensure your emails are sent from trusted servers.

The main providers are

- http://www.Aweber.com
- http://www.GetResponse.com
- http://www.MailChimp.com
- http://www.InfusionSoft.com
- http://www.iContact.com (I wouldn't use if you promote affiliate offers)

These providers vary by price and features. Also most will not let you import a lot from another provider unless they are double opt-in (a person enters their email address, the software provider sends them an email asking them to confirm they wish to receive the newsletter by clicking a link – it lowers subscribers but improves your list's quality!)

Highly Recommended...

Although I personally will recommend one above all others, http://www.Aweber.com, I have used them myself since about 2001 and built every major list I own using them (including the ones that go well into the tens of thousands) I have sent millions of emails using their service and cannot rate them high enough. I found their deliverability rate to be excellent.

I am currently testing MailChimp.com (including for this book) and seeing good results. They are easy to use and have some great features. They are also recommended.

Plus you can get even more companies you can use by joining us FREE at

www.EmailMarketingBonus.com

Autoresponders & Broadcasts

There are two types of emails you can send through the email software providers – Autoresponders and Broadcasts.

Autoresponders

Autoresponders are a series of emails you can write once and your provider will then send them out to your subscribers at the times you set.

Used correctly they are fantastic! Imagine doing the work once and then your subscribers continually get new content from you.

Example:

Day 1 – email 1 is delivered
Day 2 – email 2 is delivered
Day 4 – email 3 is delivered
Day 7 – email 4 is delivered

Day 10 – email 5 is delivered….

…Day 400 – email 60 is delivered!

You can have as many emails in your autoresponder series as you wish. You can spread them out over any time length you want.

Depending on your provider you can do clever things with autoresponders including using specific days of the week (that your provider will change automatically) and limited offers…

For example, you could write "…. You must order this by [day +3]" and in the email your customer receives, if they open it on Tuesday it would automatically say "… You must order this by Friday".

You don't want to include any date specific content in these emails e.g. "did you have a good Christmas" since depending on when someone subscribes they might receive that email in summer!

Broadcasts

These are your traditional newsletters. They are sent to your entire list regardless of when they joined.

You want to use these for 'latest news and offers' – up-to-date information.

You can segment these people if you wish and send different content to each depending on when they subscribed. You may want to write a slightly different email to your new subscribers who don't know you as well; especially if you are pitching a product.

Big Tip - I repeat this tip later in the book but it's a big tip that not many people use "You might find a good idea is to schedule all your autoresponders to be delivered on set days, perhaps Tuesday and Friday. That way it leaves Wednesday and Thursday for your mass broadcasts. Otherwise you may find that a subscriber is ending up with two different emails from you on the same day and feels a bit overloaded and may even think you're spamming them!"

Here's what you want to use...

In a word 'Both', use a smart mix of autoresponders and broadcasts to build a relationship and sell your products. For example on an old site (food making) I used to provide a load of recipes on my autoresponder, and the newsletter allowed me to sell the latest offers I had.

How Often?

Almost everyone you speak to about this will give you a different opinion on how often you should send autoresponders and newsletters.

With autoresponders you probably want to start off sending more over a short period of time and slowly lengthen the period.

For example to send 3 or 4 autoresponders in the first week is not uncommon, in the second week you might go for another 3 and in the third and fourth weeks take it down to 2 a week.

However make sure you track what your readers are doing. If you notice a lot of unsubscribers on a particular autoresponder, it will probably be one of two things:

- The content in that autoresponder is poor and you need to rewrite it.
- They are getting fed up with the volume of email and you'll want to lengthen the space between emails.

In terms of sending newsletters – how many should you send? My advice is twice a month, but you'll have other people saying once a week keeps you in the forefront of their minds, and others saying once a month works best.

Therefore I would say - write when you can provide good solid content and you have a reason to email your subscribers. There is little point writing once a week if you have nothing to say. Because over time you'll find that your subscribers simply will not respond or even bother to open your email. If however you can provide content people love then do it!

Quick Note – The exception to these would be if you were trying to get a one-time sale and have nothing else to offer (in this case, you should really rethink your business model!)

You could email every day until someone either buys or unsubscribes.

With the various email providers you can either use single or double opt-in. Again there is not a specific answer as to what is best.

A single opt-in – This is where a user enters their email address and they are automatically subscribed to your list. They don't have to take any further action.

Using this method you will get more subscribers! The downside is you'll probably get more spam complaints and it's harder to move lists between providers.

Double Opt-in - This is where someone joins your email list. But then your email provider sends them an email asking them to confirm that they really want to subscribe. Often you can customize the email that is sent. However it will cut the number of subscribers you receive since people forget to confirm or just don't get around to it.

On the plus side those who do double opt-in are more likely to be committed to reading what you send. You'll probably find you have a smaller but more responsive list.

You can help limit the number of people who 'forget or don't get around to confirming their request' by providing good instructions on your 'thank you' page. Plus if your sign up offer was really good, people should be prepared to confirm their email address because they are keen to get the offer.

In all honesty I use both. You'll note with this book it's just single opt-in. However generally I favour a double opt-in. I went for a single opt-in on this book because I didn't want to make you do more work than was needed.

Think about what your visitors are doing when they arrive at your site. In your case, you are reading the ebook or physical book. Chances are you're not near your PC.

I figure asking you to go to a single webpage and enter your email address was enough. I didn't want you then to have to open emails and confirm. It would probably be too much hassle.

You have already qualified yourself by buying the book in the first place so I'm unlikely to get too many false emails. Especially when I can help you out and improve your email marketing.

You have to realise that people are now bombarded with requests for their email address on almost every site they visit. So you have to work harder to get your visitors to hand over their email address.

The 'Lead Magnet' section is one of the most effective methods, but you still need a great reason for people to hand over their email address. We give you some great ideas in that section.

You have to answer the question "What's in it for me" why should someone give you his or her email address? What are you promising?

I'm sorry to say, especially if they are a brand new visitor, they don't really carry that much about you! They want to know how you are going to help them or what you are going to do for them.

- What problem can you solve for them?
- Can they trust you?
- Is your offer compelling?
- Make sure they can only get it from you.
- When will they receive it?

You want to try and answer all of these questions in a brief headline and a few lines of text. Look at what offers your competitors are using – how can you improve them?

Come up with the strongest benefit you can for a person to sign up and spend a while writing a headline, rewriting it – make it the strongest you can.

Tip – You may want to include something along the lines of "we'll email this report to you straight away". This is to try and stop people entering junk / false email addresses (especially important if you are using single opt-in) in the hope that they will receive your offer on the next page. If you make it clear that the offer will be emailed to them you can help limit this.

You'll want to get people to sign up to your list in any way you can think of provided they are targeted. What follows is a list of ideas you may want to integrate into your marketing to get more email subscribers outside of your website. With all the methods listed you need to give them a reason WHY!

- **Facebook** - Using iframes you can now include a subscription form inside Facebook.
- **Write a book** (like this) and include a way people can join your list.
- **Write Articles** – If you write great content that you can share with others. Include a resource box that leads to your sign up form.
- **Offering Coupons** – Offer discounts and coupons to other sites for your products. If someone clicks the link ensure they have to join your list first.
- **Affiliate programs** – Running your own affiliate scheme can generate a lot of customers. But you could also pay per subscriber (providing you can track the quality).
- **Related Companies (Not direct competitors)** – This can be effective. Set up agreements with related companies e.g. if you run a plumbing business you could do a deal with a local electrician. When someone subscribes to their list they are also given an option (and perhaps offer) to subscribe to yours and vice versa.
- **Refer a friend** – Offer an incentive for customers to refer friends to your newsletter.
- **Forums** – Provide great value to people with forum posts in topics on your niche. In your signature file include a link where they can hear more from you.
- **404 Pages** – Customize your 404 / page not found on your website to say sorry that the page no longer exists. But put an offer 'By way of an apology join our list…'

Another option is if you sell a physical product that you have to send customers. If you do, include a leaflet or some type of offer that encourages the user to go back to your website and subscribe. This can be very effective if you also sell via a third party like Amazon where you can't easily capture a customer's details.

For example if you sold 'cycling gloves' you could include a leaflet that has an offer along the lines of "Discover how you can cycle faster and further in 3 weeks with this breakthrough training technique…."

Further suggested places

How we doubled subscribers in 30 days - https://blog.bufferapp.com/get-more-email-subscribers-how-we-doubled-email-signups

17 more ways to get subscribers - http://www.lizlockard.com/get-more-subscribers-for-your-list/

Nice case study – How to go from 0 to 150,000 readers

http://andrewchen.co/early-traction-how-to-go-from-zero-to-150000-email-subscribers-guest-post/

Where can I join your list?

If that's what your visitors think - hang your head in shame!

Although I have to be honest, the company I sold one of my businesses to, now has the newsletter sign up form buried at the bottom of the home page. I bet they get a terrible response and it's costing them sales. It's madness! But that's another story.

Realistically you want to make sure EVERY visitor to your site has the chance – and not just one chance but multiple chances to join your list.

Put your sign up forms where they can't be missed!

My favourite position (and the place where I had the best response when I had forms actually on the page) was the top right. You might find top left works for you. But whatever you do please do not put it below the fold, as you will drastically harm your chances of getting a subscriber. Below the fold means making someone scroll down to see your sign up box.

Ideally you want it in this position on EVERY page of your site. If that is not possible put it there on the home page and then ensure you put a sign up box somewhere on all your other pages – preferably as high up the page as possible.

Then use the software provided by your email manager (e.g. Aweber) to give them extra chances to join.

You know you hate 'pop ups / hover over' well bad news! They work and that's why people use them! Although not as effective as they once were, they still work better than just having a plain form on your website.

Pop ups can work as follows:

- **On Entry** – As soon as a visitor arrives, a pop up email is displayed asking him/her to subscribe. These are the worst of all pop ups! Let your visitors have chance to consume your content at least for a few seconds!
- **On Exit** – As someone leaves your site you offer him/her one last chance to subscribe.

- **Fly In** – You've probably seen them, these are 'pop ups' that fly from the side of the page. They can grab attention but equally their timing should still be delayed.
- **Corner Peel** – Not quite a pop up but still in the same category. They make the top corner of your website look like it can be peeled away. When someone does that your offer or subscription box is revealed.

I would strongly test using them and 'lightboxes' (that's where you see a box pop up and the rest of the page goes dark). These can be very effective as they draw your eye to the offer.

Also test the timing of the lightboxes / popups, etc. Having it display straight away is not a good idea (generally). You want people to have a brief look at your site. Try delaying the pop up for 7 – 10 seconds and see what response you get. Try 30 seconds (most email software allows you to run split tests). The timing can have a big effect on your subscriber rate. I once increased subscribers by more than 11% by delaying the pop up for 20 seconds.

Then ideally you want to provide a 'one last chance' to subscribe and use a 'pop up on exit'. You can get some clever web scripts that will detect when a user is about to leave your website and then display your subscriber box.

You might want to look at -

http://optinmonster.com/

I've also heard good things about -

www.hellobar.com – creates a sign up bar that catches attention and goes across the top of your website.

Tip - Providing it's true, make sure you tell possible subscribers in small print just under the sign up box "We never share or sell your details". That should help increase the number of people who join.

See our own email joining page at

www.EmailMarketingBonus.com

(I may not have followed everything I've written here as I'm often testing new designs. But be sure to join and we'll share all the details with you)

Lead Magnets

I'm about to reveal one of the most under used but highly effective ways of increasing your subscribers. You want to use something called 'Lead Magnets'.

What are they?

A lead magnet is something so effective it just wants to make a visitor hand over whatever details you are asking for. Simply put it's an ethical bribe! In an extreme example if you offered a car in exchange for an email address everyone would sign up providing they believed you (and you'd be broke!) Because what you are offering in exchange for their email address is definitely worth it to them.

You want to create an offer that is so good a visitor would be crazy not to give you their email address for it. You want to try and think creatively for this because ideally you don't really want it to have a physical cost to you!

You want to create an offer that doesn't really cost you anything but has a good perceived value for your visitors. That's why you'll see so many reports, ebooks, audio and videos being given away in exchange for an email address.

You could use discount vouchers but every time someone uses it you are cutting your margins. Plus people might get wise and sign up using a few email addresses to keep getting a 10% discount (but if it works for you because you've already built that discount into your costs go for it!)

Depending on your market, can you write / record something that people really want to know about?

Tip – You'll want your lead magnet to give an immediate benefit / result. Something quick and easy for the reader to digest and get value from.

If you're giving away an ebook try and keep it simple and under 50 pages. Often a detailed 10-page report will perform better.

Often you'll find effective lead magnets have their own landing page which I'll explain in a minute.

Types of lead magnets could include:

- Product Demos
- Downloadable product catalogue (especially if you hide pricing on your webpage)
- Free trial
- Free reports
- Vouchers
- Podcasts
- Videos
- eBooks
- Loyalty program
- Webinar
- Forms e.g. quizzes
- Email sequence

Below is an example from http://joepolish.com/

It's clear and to the point, right up front on his homepage so that all his visitors see it. I would expect the conversion rate to be high, plus you have the implied extra trust with him standing next to Sir Richard Branson.

Resources on lead magnets

More on lead magnets from Infusion Soft

http://infusiontraining.s3.amazonaws.com/helpcenter/pdf-reports/10magnets.pdf

9 Lead Magnet Ideas and Examples (And ONE That Generated 28,507 Subscribers In 45 Days - http://www.digitalmarketer.com/lead-magnet-ideas-funnel/

Lead Magnets: Email List Building on Steroids - http://conversionxl.com/lead-magnets-email-list-building-on-steroids/#.

Plus you can get even more ideas by joining us FREE at

www.EmailMarketingBonus.com

Landing Pages

A landing page is the page that your visitors 'land on' – the page you want your visitors to see first!

Your landing page will have a different design and layout depending on the site your visitor has come from. For example, if you get traffic using Google Adwords then you can't use some of the most effective designs of landing pages (because Google doesn't allow you to send visitors to landing pages).

Your landing page will have a number of different functions depending on your business but I would really recommend you try and capture an email address from your visitor as many times as possible.

After all once you have their email address you can keep following them up even once they have left your website (especially using Facebook's retargeting) and it can help you increase your customers when you use Facebook's look alike audience feature! You can put them on your autoresponder list and of course send them newsletters.

Squeeze Pages

Squeeze pages are probably the most highly effective way of gathering a customer's email address. If you haven't tried them, I suggest you do.

Some marketers have 50%+ of everyone who sees the page subscribe! Imagine if you were able to get half of your visitors to give you their email address so you could follow up. Now there is an 'art' to this and getting 50%+ takes time and testing to achieve.

However I managed 45% opt-in with 100% cold traffic (e.g. they had never heard of me before) on my first attempt and I'm now testing a few ideas to increase this conversion. After all everyone who subscribes is a possible customer!

So what is a 'Squeeze Page'?

Its sole focus is to capture a person's email and maybe a few other details (e.g. name, interests, etc.)

Tip – You should try and capture a person's name and email if you can, as it will increase your open rate (more opens = more chances to sell). However the downside is that simply by asking for name and email rather than just an email address you'll hurt your conversion rate. You'll have to test and see what is better for you.

Personally I would suggest starting with a name and email. If your offer is good enough and someone wants what you are offering they should be prepared to give you the two bits of information you require. However those who are unsure probably won't!

If you start requesting too much information e.g. name, address and email it will hurt your conversion rate further.

Tip - Just gather the details that are vital to you e.g. if you run a restaurant you may want to know a person's birthday. However I would be clever and do this in a two-stage step.

On your squeeze page just ask for their email address. Once they have subscribed then send them to another page that tries to capture the other information you'd like e.g. birthday, do they use the restaurant for business or pleasure etc. That way if they aren't happy to provide you with the extra information you still have their details to follow them up with (rather than nothing at all). If you can get the extra information they become more valuable.

Remember when you present your second request for information you need to 'sell them' on why they should give you more details.

For example, using the restaurant you could offer a 'free bottle of wine' or 'free dessert' for completing the details or for their birth date.

The design of the squeeze page should be simple, no other distractions, no other calls to action. You want the sole focus to be on your signup box.

Personally I use http://www.ClickFunnels.com to manage most of my squeeze pages.

They make life really easy by providing some high converting templates that easily integrate into Aweber (my autoresponder of choice) although it works with loads of others. Since I don't know any code they manage all of that for me. It's just drag and drop stuff.

So what does a squeeze page look like?

Below are 4 examples I've taken from ClickFunnels although they do have many others (and you can even sort them by conversion rate which makes it easier).

FREE Report Reveals...

Lorem ipsum dolor sit amet, consectetur adipisicing

✔ Tortor enim euismod est, a mollis tellus magna at enim. Nullam pulvinar mi adipiscing.

✔ Tortor enim euismod est, a mollis tellus magna at enim. **Nullam pulvinar mi adipiscing.**

✔ Tortor enim euismod est, a mollis tellus magna at enim. Nullam pulvinar mi adipiscing.

Enter Your Email Address

Yes! Send Me This Free Report

🔒 We respect your privacy

This Free Report will be instantly sent to the email address you submit above.

This is one of my favourite types of squeeze page and has worked well for me in the past.

(Although if you go www.ClickFunnels.com you might see that example but equally I could be testing another design – keep testing and improving!)

I like it because you can add your logo for trust and credibility, the same as the trust logos at the top right (but as with everything on ClickFunnels you don't have to have them. You can remove / change it.)

First you have your strongest headline that should draw the customer in. I've already told you about 'lead magnets' but this is where you want your lead magnet product image. Make sure this image is strong and professional.

You subhead needs to give some more benefits followed by some brief bullet points. Pick out the main points of your product and the strongest benefit for the customer. Use the benefit not the feature in your copy.

The large red call to action really draws the eye. You don't want the visitor looking for the subscribe button.

Tip – You'll get better results by using 'Me', 'My' on your buttons rather than 'Your'. For example "Yes Send Me My Free Book" is better than "Click Here For Your Free Book".

Tip – Everyone hates spam but you'll see a lot of squeeze pages that have some text under the order button that reads, "We hate spam as much as you, we never sell or rent your details" – Don't do it! Don't put the word 'spam' in front of people as you are asking for their email address.

It's fine to say (and a good idea to reassure the visitor) by saying things like 'We respect your privacy', 'We don't share your details', etc. Just don't use the word spam!

You may think this type of squeeze page wouldn't work but it has consistently had some of the highest opt-in rates going! Plus often the background image isn't even related the content! You'll almost certainly want to test this design for yourself.

Again you've got the logo for trust and a strong headline, plus a short paragraph so you can demonstrate more benefits. The call to action button is the strongest colour on the page to draw the eye. You want your button to be the main focus.

This type of squeeze page is of more use if your traffic has heard of you before and you don't need to prove trust. For example if someone has written some great content about you on their site and is including a link. This type of squeeze page could prove effective, since the person will have already said how great you are! You just need to provide a reason for them to sign up.

Instead of using a product image you can easily use video. If you're just asking for an email address I wouldn't use video as it requires too much work on the person watching it just to give you an email address.

However if you want more information and perhaps even to schedule an appointment, a video may just be enough to presell it.

You can create an easy video simply by recording a PowerPoint presentation with some screen recorder software like Camtasia. If you prefer most smartphones have a good enough camera to record a video on.

Having a real person will probably convert better if you don't mind getting in front of the camera. You probably only want this video for a few minutes, just enough to convince the visitor to part with whatever details you require.

Discover The #1 Trick For Doubled Conversions

This Report Reveals Everything - Get Your Copy Today

> Enter Your Email Address Here...

DOWNLOAD THE FREE REPORT TODAY

" We will not spam, rent, or sell your information. "

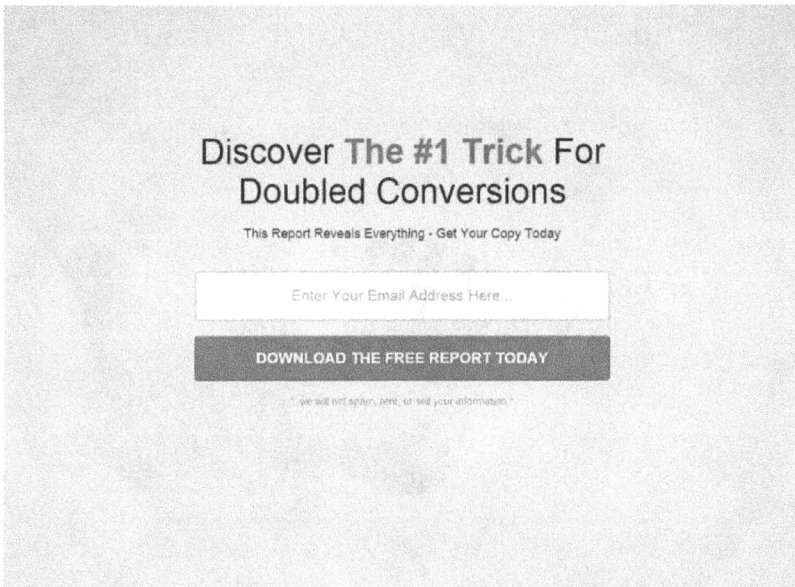

This is about as simple of squeeze page as you can get. But I've seen test results where this type of squeeze page converted the best. It tends to work best if your visitors are coming pre-recommended like from another website that has written an article on you or your own visitors who already have a relationship with you.

One very simple strong headline and the call to action. Again this can work very well on highly targeted traffic.

See our own landing page at

www.EmailMarketingBonus.com

Testing – can massively improve your results!

Consistently test your squeeze pages. To start with, test wildly different designs: try simple, try product images, video, background images, everything you can think of.

After lots of traffic you'll probably find one type of design works best for you. Then start testing different headlines, benefits, calls to action, button texts, and button colours. Basically you want to test everything you can think of.

Sometimes you'll find really bad design works best because it stands out. I read that someone had a really good professionally designed site. But simply by changing the subscriber button to bright green it increased subscribers by over 10% because it stood out!

Why?

Simply put, over time you can get better and better results with the same amount of traffic. This could mean the difference between profit and loss!

Put another away let's say you have 1000 visitors a day.

A) You currently convert at just 1% because you're not using squeeze pages or other types of opt-in to help you get subscribers. In fact, a lot of websites with just an opt-in form somewhere on their page will convert at way less than 1% but in this example it means you'll get 10 new subscribers a day.

   But then you start testing and improving…

B) By now you are using squeeze pages and popups / lightboxes and have increased your opt-in rate to 30%. That means you now have 300 new subscribers every day to build a relationship with (and of course promote offers).

Resources

Want to know more about email split testing?

5 Email A/B Split Test Ideas You Haven't Tried - http://marketingland.com/5-email-ab-split-test-ideas-you-havent-tried-49683

Three ways most marketers screw up email subject line split tests - https://econsultancy.com/blog/65569-three-ways-most-marketers-screw-up-email-subject-line-split-tests#i.n0ktexrpmfk6xs

A/B Split Testing – (some very good reading) http://www.marketingexperiments.com/improving-website-conversion/ab-split-testing.html

Plus you can get even more ideas by joining us FREE at

www.EmailMarketingBonus.com

Things your opt-in box / squeeze page must include

So that you get the highest number of people subscribing to your list you want to ensure that the squeeze page / opt-in box contains a number of elements:

- A strong headline giving the reader your No.1 benefit
- A great image – if you're giving away a report, get a graphic to reflect that, like a magazine cover. Add text to describe the offer
- Your privacy policy e.g. "Your email address will not be shared or sold"

The design and layout of your opt-in box can make or break your campaign. Just by changing the design you can double results.

As you surf the web, keep a look out for opt-in boxes that capture your attention and make a note. Either save the page or url. Keep a file so you have lots of new ideas to test.

If you need a good designer you can try places like:

- www.Fiverr.com
- www.Elance.com

There are others but those are the two sites I use all the time. Especially with Fiverr you can get new designs for just $5. If a new design can increase your subscribers by just 1% it could be worth a lot of $$ over time.

Thank You Pages

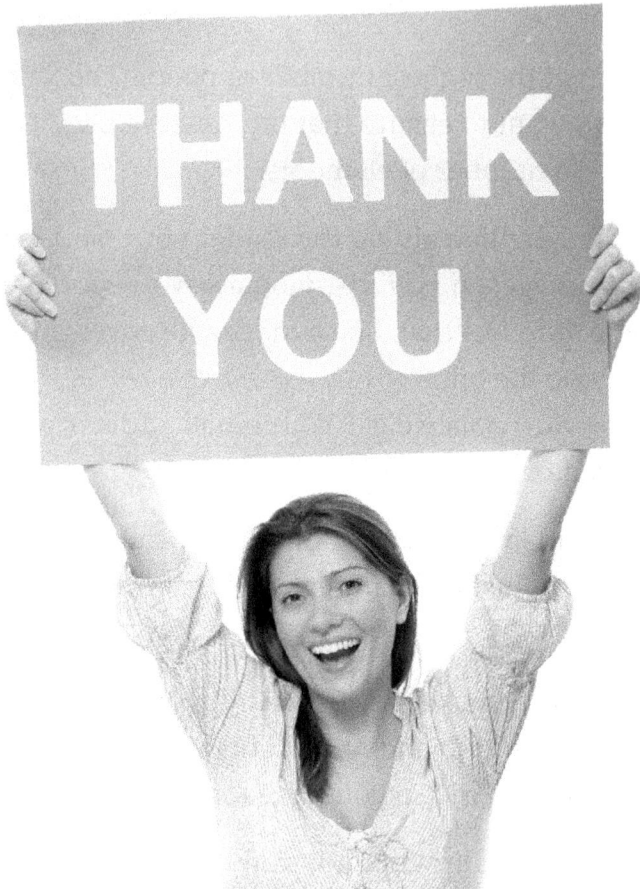

Your 'thank you page' is the page a user sees immediately after they have subscribed to your newsletter and it's very valuable.

I'm still amazed at the number of websites that just take a new subscriber back to the home page. That is such a waste of an opportunity.

This person has just taken 'action' on your website by subscribing – which is more than what most of your visitors will do. So you should do a few things for them:

Thank them for subscribing and tell them what will happen next e.g. 'Look out for an email called "WebsiteName.com – for the free report you just requested…"

If you need them to double opt-in – give instructions on what to do and what to look out for. Even better show a video or take screen grabs of each step.

But – here's what you do next….

On your 'thank you page' you should create a fantastic low priced offer that you can give your subscribers straight away.

You want to give the best value you can, even if it means you just break even. The idea is to turn as many subscribers into customers as you can.

Once you have a customer they are far more likely to purchase from you again as you have already built up some trust.

You should try and create an offer that is:

-   Low priced - $7 is ideal
-   An impulse purchase
-   Related to your main product

If you're selling software can you offer a 30-day trial for $1? – You want some type of payment so the automated rebill is set up, or at least you have card details so you can make the full price purchase after 30 days.

If you're selling a product e.g. 'fishing store' can you offer some floats or lines that are highly rated at cost price?

It's really important that you do what you can to get the customer. If nothing else it stops them from going to your competitors.

A great example of this was a guy who used to sell candle-making equipment. What is the one thing that all candle makers require? Wicks. He came up with the idea of giving them away at cost price. No one could compete with that. But once he had the customer he could then sell them wax and all the other stuff.

There was a guy who sold guitars. What was his offer? He used to sell guitar picks at cost. Anyone wanting a guitar pick probably owns a guitar and was a perfect prospect to buy a guitar in the future.

Get creative and come up with an amazing offer and you should see some great results. So many marketers miss this fantastic opportunity.

Please don't, because it will allow you to acquire more customers that hopefully you can sell to over and over again.

Whose business is more valuable?

Over the span of one year, website A has 3,650 subscribers but website B has 109,500.

A difference of 105,850 subscribers! What business would you rather own and pay more for?

What business has the greater ability to make sales and promote offers?

Which business do you think produces more profit?

Remember they didn't actually increase their visitor numbers over that time. All they did was test and improve their opt-in methods.

Although with a larger audience reading a newsletter they have a greater chance of recommendations, helping to further increase subscribers.

See how important testing is and yet most business owners fail to do it which to be honest I just don't understand. You work hard to get visitors and sales and yet failing to test you could be losing a lot of potential customers.

You can test easily with ClickFunnels.com but there are some other great testing software resources around like Optimizely.com and VWO.com –

Please just start testing. Most of you reading this intend to but won't!

How often should you email?

In short when you think a customer wants to hear from you. What did you originally promise?

If you said join our 'weekly newsletter' stick to that. Don't go and do it twice a week or monthly. You build up a following by building trust!

However if you didn't promise any schedule you need to think about what your aim is.

What day and time are best to send your email?

You want to do everything you can to maximize the number of people who open your email. The more opens you have, the more chances you have of them taking the action you want.

The day you send your email can have a big impact on your open rate. You need to think whom you are targeting most and who your readers are. For example if your mailing list is mostly business emails then sending a newsletter at 9 pm on a Friday night will be next to useless.

GetResponse analysed their email stats and found that most emails were sent on a Thursday. But equally Thursday had the highest engagement rate as well.

Top sending days were:

1 – Thursday (highest)

2 – Wednesday

3 – Friday

4 – Tuesday

5 – Monday

6 – Saturday

7 – Sunday (lowest)

However click through rates went from:

1 – Thursday (highest)

2 – Tuesday

3 – Friday

4 – Wednesday

5 – Monday

6 – Saturday

7 – Sunday

Tip – You might find a good idea is to schedule all your autoresponders to be delivered on set days, perhaps Tuesday and Friday. That way it leaves Wednesday and Thursday for your mass broadcasts.

Otherwise you may find that a subscriber is ending up with two different emails from you on the same day and feel a bit overloaded and may even think you're spamming them!

Think about your customers...

For my ecommerce website I always used to send on a Tuesday 10:30 am. The reason was that it gave everyone Monday to get over the weekend and focus on work.

By Tuesday people are more easily distracted (which is what I wanted!!) and they will visit the website and order.

By ordering on a Tuesday there was a good chance their order would arrive by Wednesday or Thursday (Friday at the latest) which gave the impression of great service = happy customer.

Had I sent the email at 2 pm on Thursday, by the time people ordered and we packed the order, it wouldn't have been ready to send until after our courier had arrived and gone. Meaning orders wouldn't have left us until Friday and that meant orders would not arrive to customers until Monday, Tuesday or even Wednesday. The weekend made it feel like delivery was slow.

What is your expectation of sending the email? What do you want to accomplish with the email? Then work it back as to what schedule will work best for you.

Times

As well as the day you send your email, the time of day can have an impact. For example, 9 am on a Monday is probably not the best time to ask someone for a commitment! They've just walked into work and are probably thinking about the mountain of work they need to get through and don't have the time to deliberate your offer.

However on another day, later in the day they might be flagging and your offer can capture their attention.

A lot of studies have been published on when is the best time of day to email your list.

GetResponse analysed 21 million emails to work out the top sending and engagement times. They found when you send your email matters a lot!

Here's what they found

The best times of day for sending a newsletter were 8 am – 10 am and 3 pm – 4 pm. That can increase open rates by 6%.

Hour by hour…

1st hour – 23.63% of all opens

2nd hour – 9.52%

3rd hour – 6.33%

4th hour – 4.8%

22nd hour – 0.78%

23rd hour – 0.72%

24th hour – 0.63%

Notes – Emails have their best results within the 1st hour. After just one hour open rates fall by half, and drop another 30% in the 3rd hour.

Also consider what your readers are doing at the time you send. GetResponse found that an email sent at 5 pm had a 23.63% chance of being opened.

But then – what next…

Your potential customers leave work, travel home, eat dinner, get their children to bed, catch up with family and friends… by now 3 or 4 hours have passed and your open rate is less than 5%.

Most emails arrive in an inbox in the morning. You have all the emails that arrived since you looked the night before and then you have new emails arriving that require your attention.

That's why emails that arrive 'in the afternoon' have the best chance of being noticed, opened and clicked.

GetResponse found the top click hours were:

8 am – 9 am and 3 pm – 8 pm

Top open hours:

8 am – 9 am and 3 pm – 4 pm

Note – Depending on the size of your list and your software provider it can take several hours for all your emails to be sent. So schedule that in to your calculations. However if you are using the top providers like Aweber, GetResponse, and MailChimp you should find that they can send tens of thousands of emails for you within an hour or two.

What I found…

Although I have only sent a few million emails during my time running an ecommerce store I had the best results sending around 10:30 in the morning. That way most emails were at people's desks as they started lunch.

I wanted people to see the email and then browse my store as they ate lunch. By delaying until 2 pm and later my sales from the newsletter went down as people had less time to engage – even though the open rates were still fairly constant.

Think what action you want people to take. If you are sending a newsletter that is just that 'news' then following GetResponse may well work best for you.

People can sit at a work PC and read a 'private' email much easier than if you are expecting them to click a link and browse an ecommerce store or watch a video, something they could more easily do on their lunch hour.

Tip – from that point of view it's also worth considering your email content. By going easy on graphics, photos and html it's much easier to read a non work email whilst sitting at your desk.

But if your email loads with 'Big Sale' in big red letters then anyone walking past knows that person isn't working. So whilst you may get the open, they'll probably hit delete straight away.

Importance of Your List

A lot of business owners will tell you **"the money is in the list"** and to a certain extent that is true.

Without a list of customers or people interested in your service it's hard to remarket to them or even convert them in the first place. Remember it often takes 7 contact points before you get a customer. Therefore if you have no way of following up with a customer you lose lots of opportunities to make the sale.

But having a huge list will not necessarily do the trick. Just to prove a point if you are selling kitchens, what would you rather have

1 – A list of 500 people interested in home renovation?

Or

2 – A list of 10,000 people interested in fishing?

Sure a small percentage of the people in list 2 may be interested in buying a new kitchen but chances are it will be much harder to sell to these people. You always want to make sure you are building a highly targeted list.

It's the relationship you have with your list that will make you the money.

In all honesty I'd take a list of 50 subscribers all interested in home renovation if every time I sent an email it had a 100% open and click through rate. These people are clearly more interested in what you are offering.

You want to work hard on 'Building the Relationship' with anyone on your list. Treat your list with respect and you can make a lot of money from it by building relationships.

They may not buy from you on the first contact. But keep in touch and keep giving them value and over time you should get their trust so that when you do pitch an offer they are interested and you stand a good chance of making a sale.

That means don't simply send email after email for the sake of it. Make sure every email you write has something of value, something that someone wants to read. Use it to build up your trust and authority with the reader so they respect you.

Who are you more likely to buy from?

1 – Someone you trust and have a relationship with

2 – The sales person you know is trying to sell you something

You can get to be the person in the first category by providing value.

Extra Tip – If you can and your market allows it, make your emails personal so you stand out from the crowd. I used to have a very popular hobby product and in the emails I sent to customers I would often mention stuff that the kids and I had been doing. It made us seem like a genuine business (which we were) but it was different from our competitors who were simply pitching a product every time.

If you're selling fishing gear tell your readers what your latest trip was, what you caught, how the equipment performed. Don't be afraid of saying it's rubbish when it is. Again you'll build trust and respect. Everyone knows not all products are great.

I'm a member of a marketing list and the writer is always saying what he's done at the weekend. I even know that he suffered a heart attack earlier in the year and now has panic attacks. He's also currently moving to a new house. He tells me which latest marketing products he thinks are rubbish and others that are great. He has built my trust over time and I now respect his opinions. I am much more likely to buy from him because I feel I know him a bit and trust him.

You need to prove to readers you are someone real and not some faceless business. There is no better way than telling real stories and sharing photos to help build up the relationship.

Tips for a Better Email

You'll find after testing, a few things can have a big impact on your emails. But you'd be wise to follow a few simple rules when putting together your emails:

Use lots of white space

Use short sentences

Use short paragraphs – 2 or 3 sentences is fine. It's not an English test.

Don't use 'complicated' words.

Make it easy to read and scan. You want readers to be able to get a gist of your email straight away.

One of the biggest no no's is using templates. A lot of providers will give you some flashy templates. As soon as one of these arrives in your inbox you know straight away that it's a commercial and you put up your defences!

Please use a spell checker.

Tip – Go and sign up for a free email account at Yahoo, Gmail, and Hotmail. Then make sure you send a test email to those accounts and make sure the format looks right.

You might want to try - https://litmus.com/email-testing (paid service) to see how your email looks on different platforms.

Often you'll need to put double line breaks in emails to make them look right on all email platforms. Otherwise in some people's email readers your email will appear without any line breaks and become almost impossible to read.

Make sure you test EVERY link on your email. I learnt that the hard way.

If you must include images make sure they are optimized / compressed for faster loading. I'd also link any images to whatever page you want people to click to.

Subject Lines

With your readers scanning down a huge list of emails that they receive every day deciding which ones to open, your subject line is one of the most important elements of your entire email. Get that wrong and your email will fail before it's even opened.

You probably know yourself that you don't open nearly all the email you receive. How do you decide? As you scan down the list you are looking for headlines that grab your attention and raise your interest. If it looks uninteresting or boring you simply skip over it and never return.

You need to work hard to come up with a headline that will stand out.

According to the brilliant marketer Ryan Deiss of DigitalMarketer.com he says every subject line should have at least 1 of these 7 elements:

- **Self Interest**
  Probably one of the best ways to get an open is to communicate a big benefit – what will the email do for the reader? Will it give them something they want or something they wish to avoid?

- **News**
  Everyone wants to know something newsworthy.

- **Curiosity**
  These are really hard to get right. Do it and they can be the most effective lines you'll write. Get it wrong and they'll probably give you the lowest open rates. Can you combine this element with another element?

- **Social Proof**
  Experiments time after time have shown that people tend to like following what others have done. Can you prove a great result from what others have experienced?

- **Urgency**

Can you give a reason to act now? Is something going to expire, sell out…

-   **Story**
    The headline that starts to tell a story can be very effective.

-   **Humanity**
    People like doing business with people they like!

But Don't

Don't make your subject lines clever. Making your reader work to understand your headline isn't going to work. They need to grasp what you are saying instantly.

Examples

So let's give you some examples of great headlines that you can adapt to suit your market:

"… Best Seller in 4 Days"

It promises a benefit in a specific amount of time

"….Closing Down"

Curiosity and self-interest, they might be about to miss out on something good.

"13 ways you can…."

Being specific and with self interest

"I made an awful mistake, here's how to…"

Curiosity as to what has happened and you're going to show readers how not to make the same mistake as you.

"You're missing out on…."

Don't be shy in letting people know they are about to miss a great deal.

"Where to" & "How to"

These subject lines always tend to grab the attention.

"As promised, here's the additional information you need"

Implies that they already requested something, and are going to need whatever is included in the email.

You can group headlines in to a few topics.

Questions

"How much will this…"

"Have you reached…."

"Want even more…"

"What's the…"

"Who's the most…"

"What do…"

Urgent

"Only 4 left…."

"It's being taken down for good at…"

"Hurry, only 3 days until…"

"Ends today at…"

"Last chance to…"

"Last minute deals to…"

"Act now to…"

"Your deadline is…"

"Final notice"

Offers

"Free upgrade if you…"

"Don't miss this limited free…"

"Get my … totally free when you…"

"Grab your free…"

"Highly recommended free…."

"7,679 have already been given away free, last few…"

"Extended for you by 24 hours…."

"Take your pick of…"

Interesting

"They went too far and…"

"Even a newbie can…"

"The true secrets of how you can…"

"The must read formula to…"

"If I had to start again, this is what I'd do…"

"Listen to this if you want to…"

"Exclusive just for you and…."

"How to get… for …."

"Revealed, how to…"

Product Sales

"Just arrived…"

"Be the first to own…"

"You could be enjoying this in 16 hours…"

"Our best selling… is almost gone for good…"

"30% off because we had a disaster in…"

"Enjoy this special offer…"

"Save 30% when you…"

"Introducing our latest…"

Events

"Join us when we…"

"We are about to go live and we're waiting for you…"

"Our biggest event ever and we are going to…"

Negative

"Don't buy … because…"

"Warning, please watch out for these top…"

"It's awful…"

"They lied to us about…"

Numbers

"7 ways to…"

"13 reasons to…"

"6 great tips"

"Top 10 most…"

"87 improvements you can make…"

"Only 2 remaining…"

"8 ideas to…"

You may want to test using additional characters in your subject headlines. If they can stop a reader scrolling down their list of emails and get them to click on your email they've done their job. You could try things like

F | R | E | E gift if you….

[today only] Open today and you'll…

Have you seen…. {newsletter name}

"oh yes…" speech marks might proof useful, especially if you are telling a story

#1 way to increase….

Personally I haven't used the top example (because I think it looks spammy) but I have used variations of the other 4 examples with success. It can help interrupt the eye flow and get a reader's attention.

A few other points to remember

Using capital letters in your email subject header increases readership "Have You Seen These…" is better than "Have you seen these…"

If you have the reader's name – use it! Again it increases the chances they'll open your email by about 22% so if you can "Tom – Have You Seen These…" would be a great strategy to use.

Resources

If you want more ideas you may want to read http://blog.crazyegg.com/2014/01/29/email-subject-line-hacks/

Book readers - bit.ly/1kSwe9R

Another great resource – 100 of the best headlines ever written http://www.mastercopywriters.com/greatestheadlines.htm

See how you can rewrite some of those for your own market.

Write Effective Subject Lines - http://kb.mailchimp.com/delivery/deliverability-research/write-effective-subject-lines

Subject Line Spam Trigger Words - http://www.mequoda.com/articles/audience-development/subject-line-spam-trigger-words/

The 17 Best Email Subject Lines for Increasing Open Rates [+ Video] - http://www.mequoda.com/articles/audience-development/best-email-subject-lines/

9 great ways to start your email

MicksGarage.com	This Email Contains No Gimmicky Offers... Just Permanently Lower Prices! - Free shipping on all orders over £50? Can't see the images in this mail? Click Here to view in
Eben Pagan	The "Launch Guru" SPEAKS - If you have been watching all of these million dollar launches online, and thinking to yourself that
Jay Boyer and John S. Rh.	I ruffled some feathers yesterday... Well I seem to have created somewhat of a fanfare with my email yesterday (thanks for your feedback
Stuart Walker	65 High Paying Affiliate Programs That Pay $100-$5,000 Commission - Hey buddy, If you're fed up of getting ripped off by Amazons measly 4% commission rate and not
Brendon Burchard	please read today for prep - I've been sharing with you many of the secrets that helped me promote
Zoe at PeoplePerHour	The new F word changing the way we work! - PeoplePerHour.com Meet Our Sellers PPH Tips Hello alan, A focus on quality has always been at the
Jeff Johnson	how I turned a crappy sales letter into a new business - Back in December of 2005, just a couple of days before Christmas, I decided to open up my first paid
Brian Moran (2)	[Sale] My personal Facebook "swipe files" - What a stunning experience that was for me. The very first time I sat down at my computer after
The HOTH	Our BIG SEO Giveaway - We're giving away $900+ worth of SEO Goodies Dudes and Dudettes, Continuing our Customer

When you send an email, most email clients now display the first few words or even the first few lines of the email you sent.

Since people often receive tens or hundreds of emails a day. **"If you are anything like me you scan down the emails and only open the ones that interest you."**

Along with the email subject line you need to make the opening words and sentences really count.

Getting this right can really help improve your open rate. It's vital that you spend a bit of time getting this right.

After you've got their attention using a great headline don't let yourself down by using a poor choice of words for the beginning of your email. Forget the bland, spend time coming up with something creative. What can you write that would make you want to know more?

"Good news"

Simple and effective, everyone loves to hear good news. Let them know straight away you have some good news for them.

"I have an answer for you"

Simply implies you've done some work for them and have an answer to their question. Everyone loves answers to questions and this is just making it easy for them.

"I'll be honest with you"

Meaning you'll tell the truth whilst some other people may not.

"It's starting now"

Readers often don't want to miss something and this is a good introduction to something that is just about to happen.

"Urgent"

Makes people pay attention, although it is getting really over used in business marketing.

"I'm really sorry"

Again all about curiosity, people love to know what went wrong. Especially when your email implies it was your fault.

"The rumours are true"

They'll think what rumours? But chances are they'll want to know what other people have been hearing.

"Just getting back to you"

Simple and effective (and also overused so be aware) but they'll think what are they getting back to me about?

Make sure your opening sentences do not mislead. Otherwise you'll put your readers on edge right from the start. They'll think straight away they've been tricked and from there no matter what you say, it will be hard to recover and get them to take the action you want.

What should you write about?

You probably know this area better than any book could teach you. But at some point you'll almost certainly get writers block for new content. If you do, try these suggestions for ideas:

- http://answers.yahoo.com
- http://alltop.com
- Article sites like http://ezinearticles.com
- www.wikianswers.com
- www.answers.com
- http://www.quora.com – find questions / answers on your topic
- Search Google for your niche + forum
- Search Google for your niche + blog
- Look at your old newsletters, can you rewrite, improve, update old content?

Tip – A method that always worked well for me was including some type of quiz in the newsletter (true / false etc.) with the reader having to click a link to go to a page on my site for the answers. Of course on the 'answers' page I also reinforced the offer I was making in that email. It helped get people to revisit the site.

Tip – Always tease what is coming in the next newsletter e.g. "look out for my email next week where I'll show you exactly how you can…" You get the idea. The same way TV shows often leave you with a cliff hanger. You want to try and do the same in your emails.

While you are writing your emails always try and show who you are and use your personality to build up a relationship with your reader.

I know I've said it a few times in the book, but I really want to stress how important it is to build a relationship with your readers so they feel they can trust you. Then when you make recommendations they feel you are an expert and trustworthy and they will hopefully take action, rather than just thinking you are trying to sell them something.

So when you are writing always try and include a few topics like:

- What you've been doing
- What you're looking forward to
- What your kids are up to
- Stuff that you found funny (be careful not make any offensive jokes)
- Things that make you cross
- Give opinions on topics

It's also worth remembering if you are going to run a 'Fathers Day' or 'Mothers Day' promotion (especially if you have a good relationship with your list) be careful how you pitch it. I always used to say something like "If you're lucky enough to still have your Mother…" before going on. I learnt that at my cost when once I didn't and a few people complained that they had just lost their parent.

At the end of the day people buy things from people they like, know and trust.

Keep track of your emails

Email	opened	clicked	bounced	complaints
{!firstname_fix} New Wasgij (3) Have just arrived.... View Stats | Copy Sent to 47,721 subscribers at 06/13/14 07:18 AM Includes **1 additional lists** .	10.5k	0	247	10
{!firstname_fix} May jigsaw offer and did you see.... View Stats | Copy Sent to 47,901 subscribers at 05/13/14 05:36 AM Includes **1 additional lists** .	9.9k	0	177	11
{!firstname_fix} Some lovely jigsaw images I think.... View Stats | Copy Sent to 48,128 subscribers at 04/29/14 05:31 AM Includes **1 additional lists**	10.5k	0	213	14
{!firstname_fix} FREE Puzzle Board Sorter (Special... View Stats | Copy Sent to 48,285 subscribers at 04/08/14 05:27 AM Includes **1 additional lists** .	11.3k	0	183	8
{!firstname_fix} Can you spare 2 minutes please? View Stats | Copy Sent to 48,451 subscribers at 03/19/14 06:54 AM Includes **1 additional lists** .	13k	0	257	7

You'll want to keep track of the emails you send. Over time you should build up a good number of subscribers and start to get some good data on what is and isn't working.

Then when you send an email make sure you look at the statistics afterwards.

- What was the open rate?
- What was the click through rate?
- Unsubscribe rate?
- How does it compare to previous emails?
- Were the statistics in line with previous emails?

If you notice a fall in open rates or click through rates see if you can find the cause. Poor offer, poor subject, not as much content as before.

Often as your list grows the open and click through rates will fall slightly. But you should be getting at least 20% open rate and 7% click through rate even when sending tens of thousands.

Note – I never used to track my click throughs using the autoresponder.

Why?

Because I preferred sending a text based email (and often had best results that way) if I used Aweber tracking it used to change the link from

Mywebsite.com/greatoffer

To something like

Aweber.com/g82bb8nas9sn009ss0

I thought it took trust away and made the link look spammy! I would rather my readers saw my web address which they knew and trusted rather than some strange looking url.

I learnt this the hard way – I once sent a newsletter using tracking url's and noticed afterwards that the click through rate was way below normal.

I then ran a split test on the next newsletter and the normal url newsletter had a 141% better click through rate. That was massive and therefore I never again used tracking urls in email newsletters.

How to use Email Really Effectively in Your Business

Depending on the email software you use you can do some very clever things with email and autoresponders.

Win Back Old Customers

Here's a great way you can win back old customers. Say you have a product (let's use dress patterns in this example) and your average repeat order rate is every 3 months. If after 4 months the customer hasn't reordered you should do your best to try and bring them back.

They've already been a customer of yours once and provided you delivered a good service there is no reason why you can't get a repeat order from them. Especially since you have all their contact details you should definitely be in contact.

Because they haven't yet reordered you will probably need to offer these customers some type of incentive for taking action – think free gift, discount etc. but also include an 'urgency' about it so you try to encourage them to take action straight away.

Below are a few possible subject lines. If you can, use the person's name to try and engage them and show that the email was sent to them (rather than a mass newsletter). Even if they don't want the offer it's a useful way to make sure there wasn't any problem.

Even if they email back and say 'everything's fine…' it's still an engagement and a small action they took towards you.

Subject: [Name] We've missed you, here's 30% off just for you
Subject: [Name] It's been too long, here's a special gift just for you
Subject: [Name] Just wanted to give you our best ever…
Subject: [Name] Are you ok? Because I just wanted to give you….

Email Body

Hi [Name]

I just wanted to check and make sure everything is ok. I was looking at our records just now and noticed that you ordered (product name) about 3 months ago but we haven't heard from you since. Was everything ok?

Hoping you just forgot about us and I'd really like to have you back. So I decided to create a special gift for you. Please take a look at xxxxx and if you see anything you like I'll give you 30% off simply if you use this code.... Or if you prefer you can get x for x plus I'll get your order sent straight away so you can have it tomorrow.

It's a crazy offer and I'm only going to keep it open until xxxx as stock is really limited.

But the truth is I just want you back as a customer. If there is anything we can do to help please just get in contact.

Best wishes
[Your Name]

P.S. Include some great PS to reconfirm your offer

Asking For Reviews

Another great autoresponder is to help you get reviews. Reviews are so important now. If you're selling on Amazon you need your product to have lots of positive reviews (and probably more than the competition) to win the sale. If you're offering a service you'll need reviews on the popular review sites like 'TripAdvisor'.

Now be warned that incentivizing reviews is strictly against the terms and conditions of almost all review sites. You also can't ask for positive reviews!

But you are allowed to ask for a review (although do check the terms and conditions of what site you want the reviews for) and provided you believe in the product or service you offer and that people will be pleased with it; there's no reason not to ask for the review.

By getting more positive reviews than your competitors you can really start to outsell / get more customers than they have.

Subject: [Name] Please can you do me a quick favour?

Body –

Hi [Name]

About 2 weeks ago you purchased [product name] from me. I really hope you found it useful. It's tough being a small business at the moment and I'd appreciate it if you could spend just 2 minutes and help me out?

Please could you leave me a quick review at [website name] just saying what you thought? I'd be ever so grateful and it would help me out massively. It really will only take about 2 minutes.

Of course if you have any questions, problems etc. then I'm always here to help. Please just get in contact.

Best wishes

[Your Name]

P.S. If you could leave the review at [website name] – thank you again.

TIP – This is the type of autoresponder you'll need to change probably every week to change the location of where you want your review left. If you have 100 reviews at TripAdvisor and none anywhere else it could lead to problems. Decide on the sites that are important and then just change the autoresponder weekly.

Also it does no harm to follow up a week or so later. I used to do this very effectively. Since it would be hard to check if each person left a review and at what location I used to use a generic email quite effectively and out of thousands sent I don't recall one compliant!

"Hi [Name]

I'm really sorry I've been so busy packing orders, I haven't had a chance to check if you were able to leave me a review. If you were 'thank you' so much it really does help us a lot. You probably checked out our reviews first before buying so you know how important they are.

If you haven't yet please would you kindly do it at [website name] it will only take 2 minutes and I would be really appreciative. We work hard to try and deliver a good service and letting people know is hard. These reviews are so important.

As always any questions please just email me.

Best wishes

[Your name]

Year Anniversary

If something you sell is often purchased for a gift or at a set interval then it would be a good idea to include an email about 50 / 51 weeks after the first sale. Whatever it was that was purchased a year ago might be appropriate again this year.

Or if you didn't get the sale last year, simply by sending a reminder email again this year might be enough to get the sale. It doesn't cost you anything (apart from your email costs) and can be an effective way to win back previous customers.

Thank You / Congratulations

A simple 'thank you' email can work really effectively. You could send it a few days after a first order or renewing a service.

This one was a favourite of mine when I used to sell physical products. Along with the receipt email we'd also send an email giving the customer another 10% off any order within the next 30 days. We had a really good take up on it.

Subject: [Name] Thank you very much, here's your….

Body –

Hi [Name]

I just wanted to say thank you again for your order yesterday. I'm pleased to say it's already on it's way and if not delivered already it will be with you very soon. Hope you'll be very happy with it.

Just as an extra 'thank you' I wanted to give you a 10% off voucher than you can use anytime in the next 30 days (and as many times as you want) on any of our products.

As you checkout please just use the code 'myspecialthankyou' and you'll save 10% straight away.

Not sure if you noticed but we just had some great new [products] delivered that have proved very popular.

Anyway, thank you again. Please if you have any questions just get in contact. I'm here to help.

Best wishes,

[Your name]

Buying Mailing Lists

This is a trap many new marketers fall into. I would strongly suggest you avoid it at all costs and I'll explain why.

There are many companies on the web that will sell you a mailing list on almost any topic you want. If you want a list of hotel owners you can get it, a list of plumbers no problem, you can even get lists of people who have connected with various topics on Facebook. The problem is in how the emails were collected.

Most companies providing these lists simply scrape the web for email addresses. This means they write a piece of software that scans websites for email addresses on various topics and then combines them into one large database that they will sell you.

For example, if you want a list of 'hotel owners in New York' the software would generally go out and search Google for 'New York Hotels'. It would go through the thousands of results saving each and every email address it finds.

Now I can understand it can be tempting to purchase a list rather than building your own because it's far quicker but the consequences can be harsh.

The Honey Trap

(No not that kind of honey!)

A lot of internet service providers want to stop spam emails. Let's face it no one wants to read spam emails. It's bad for the user experience so a lot of providers use what they call a 'honey trap'.

They will purposely create fake email addresses for both private individuals and businesses throughout the web. Then a bit of software comes along and collects one or more of these addresses. You have absolutely no way of knowing which email address is real or fake. These emails are then combined into huge lists that are sold to unknowing consumers and businesses.

Here's what happens next...

You, being the innocent business owner, buy a list of 'hotel owners in New York' but included in that list are one or more of these 'honey trap' email addresses. When you send out your bulk emails you'll send an email to one of these fake addresses.

When that happens they'll know you have bought / used software to collect these email addresses and no matter how great your email you'll be marked as a 'spammer'.

This results in ALL your emails being labelled as spam. Not just on this mailing but potentially on all future mailings! All because you sent an email to a 'honey trap' email address.

If you do, it will be a pain to try and get your email address white listed again.

Are you blacklisted?

If you have bought or harvested emails in the past you may have already been blacklisted. That could be the reason why your emails have had a terrible response. It may be you did it years ago without knowing. Whatever the reason it is worth checking every few weeks that your server is not blacklisted.

There are a few online places you can check:

http://www.spamhaus.org/lookup/

http://mxtoolbox.com/blacklists.aspx

http://www.blacklistalert.org/

Other ways to get blacklisted

Whilst sending bulk unsolicited email is probably the easiest way to get blacklisted. You can get blacklisted for a number of other reasons. The top two are:

- High number of bounced / undelivered emails
- High number of spam complaints

You need to ensure you keep your list clean. By that I mean removing subscribers who never open your emails or bounce.

Simply having a high bounce rate can start to affect the deliverability of the rest of your email campaigns.

Spam

You know what spam is, those unsolicited emails that keep appearing in your inbox. Most email providers are now doing a fairly good job of filtering out that rubbish. But of course it means that it makes it harder for you to market to customers. Why? Because often, genuine emails are labelled as spam or Google puts them into its promotions tab!

Make sure you offer unsubscribe links in every email – why?

Every email you send to your list must have an unsubscribe link and you must make it clear, don't hide it.

After I ended my email I usually added about 6 return keys and then the 'unsubscribe' link would appear. I did that for 2 reasons:

- The unsubscribe link was clearly there for anyone who wanted to use it
- By putting 6 return key strokes between the end of my email message (just after the P.S.) I made sure no one clicked it by mistake e.g. they wanted to click my link but weren't paying attention and carelessly went to unsubscribe!

Remember you don't want anyone on your list that doesn't want to read your email. It's better to have 100 readers who love your content than 10,000 who never open it!

Spend your time building relationships with your readers!

0.5% of your subscribers could harm you – or 1 in 200.

Yes that's all it takes to label you as a spammer! If just 1 in 200 readers click the 'report as spam' button you could be in trouble with your email provider and you'll find your deliverability rate goes through the floor.

So before you start 'selling' make sure you work on building the relationship and creating value. If you go straight for the 'big sell' and readers report you as spam you will not get another chance to make the sale! So it's better to take a softer approach.

Most email providers like Aweber, MailChimp etc. will automatically manage your unsubscribe requests.

Plus you can get even more tips by joining us FREE at

www.EmailMarketingBonus.com

Avoiding Google's Promotions Tab + Spam Filters

Google added a 'promotions' tab to its Gmail users' mailbox with the intention of filtering out all promotional emails! Well thanks! It just made your job much harder. They really don't want their users to read your sales messages!

Although if you are in a very competitive market it can actually work to your advantage. If you can get your email delivered to the 'inbox' while all of your competitors emails end up in the 'promotions' folder you can massively increase your readership.

The most obvious way of avoiding the 'promotions' tab is to ask your readers to tell Gmail to deliver it to your inbox.

They can do it by marking your emails as 'primary' or dragging them to the 'inbox'. But in reality this is next to useless. The only people who will do that have already seen your email and are prepared to do it. 99% of readers, even if they find it in the 'promotions' tab, will not drag it across (unless of course you are providing exceptional value to them).

What you really want is for your email to land in the 'inbox' from the start.

Here's the secret that will help you land your emails in the 'inbox' more often:

- Include only 1 link per email
- No pictures
- Use the reader's name (which most email software will allow easily)
- Write an email like you are writing to a friend
- Avoid html code

Think about it, all of that makes perfect sense. Google wants to deliver email from friends, not sales messages.

What friend do you have that writes using the same link 3 or 4 times throughout their email, then includes a few graphics and possibly bolds words and writes in a sale tone? It's fairly easy to filter that out.

Again it goes back to what I've said about treating the reader as a 'friend'. Write to them in the same way and you should have a much higher readership rate as well because your emails are not being filtered out.

Spam filters work in the same way trying to filter out unwanted email. The more you can make your emails appear as if they are from a friend and less 'salesy' the greater the chance you have of making it through.

Repeated use of words like:

- Free
- Limited
- Offer
- Sale
- Click Now

are all signs of a classic commercial email and are easy to detect. When was the last time a friend emailed you a link and said, "click now"?

Can-Spam Act

In most countries now there are laws that you must be aware of in regards to sending email. Make sure you are aware of the laws in your country and any laws that apply to you from other countries where you send email.

I suggest you read -

http://www.business.ftc.gov/documents/bus61-can-spam-act-compliance-guide-business

Points to note in every email you send you should (but not limited to)

- Have an easy 'unsubscribe' link so anyone who no longer wants to receive your emails can remove their details
- Have a physical address in your email (normally put at the bottom of your emails)
- A clear disclosure of any affiliate relationship or advertising
- A message that says how and when the subscriber joined, ip address used

Canada is also introducing some tough new anti spam measures which you can read about

http://fightspam.gc.ca/eic/site/030.nsf/eng/home

Or a simpler version
http://www.copyblogger.com/casl-2014/

Great case studies

You'll want to watch these from
http://www.marketingexperiments.com/

1 - http://www.marketingsherpa.com/article/case-study/obama-email-campaign-testing - How the Obama campaign generated approximately $500 million in donations from email marketing

2 - http://www.marketingsherpa.com/article/case-study/testing-subject-line-symbols - Email Marketing: Cold testing subject line symbols leads to increased open rates for health care company

3 - http://www.marketingexperiments.com/blog/research-topics/email-marketing/optimize-campaign.html - 3 resources to help you optimize your next campaign

4 - http://www.marketingexperiments.com/blog/research-topics/email-marketing/copywriting-test-increases-clickthrough.html - Copy test increases click through 37%

((⏺ AWeber

I've already said how much I like Aweber.com and why I have used it for why over 10 years. I also believe that in writing this book it's my job to give you the best information possible, which is why I wanted to share this super powerful trick I learnt about via

http://www.smartpassiveincome.com/a-ninja-email-autoresponder-trick-you-can-use-to-save-time-and-make-more-money/

Book readers - bit.ly/ZBU1FQ

The above page includes step-by-step screen shots for you to make it super easy. Although this section isn't big please take the time to read and understand it. It can be incredibly powerful.

Once you have your autoresponder list in place you can keep in contact with your loyal readers on a regular basis building up trust and credibility. But if you've set them up right you are going to have a huge number of autoresponders going out to your subscribers and customers for a variety of reasons. I think in one list I had over 40 follow ups alone!

But what happens when you want to promote a new product, launch a new service or run a webinar? It would take hours to go in and type a promo at the bottom of each email (not to mention how dull that would be).

But there is an easier way....

How would you like to include a call to action that at anytime you can change and it will dynamically change them in all your emails at once?

This is massive and done right is a huge tip but Aweber allows you to dynamically insert what they call 'Global Text Snippets'. (I don't think other services allow you to do this.)

At the bottom of each of your autoresponders if you include a 'Global Text Snippet' it will allow you to promote whatever you want at the bottom of all your autoresponders and then change it whenever you like with a new offer.

For example if you are promoting a clearance item you could include a mention of it at the bottom of every email you send. But then once you've sold out you can then change it to a new offer. Instead of it taking hours to change 40 emails you can do it in minutes.

Sign Up To Your Competitors and Buy Something

Make sure you get on all of your competitors' newsletters as well. I would strongly suggest using different email addresses so they can't connect it to you. Plus sign up as 'pre-customer' and see what emails you are sent. Then make a purchase using a different email address and see what emails you receive. There are a few benefits to this:

- Not only will it give you content ideas for your own emails, you can use their emails as a basis for your own if you want but just improve on what they offer.
- You can see if / how they are targeting offers between customers and pre-customers.
- You'll discover what they are planning, any offers they are running, so you can compete against them if you wish.

If nothing else it's great competitor intelligence. If you are interested in knowing more about what your competitors do here are some tools that might help:

- https://www.google.com/alerts
- https://www.changedetection.com/
- http://www.keywordspy.com/research/
- Plus an overview - http://www.inc.com/guides/201105/10-tips-on-how-to-research-your-competition.html

Some clever email marketing with Facebook!

Most people don't know about this – let alone use it. But yet it can be very, very effective in helping to increase customers and subscribers.

Saving the best for last... Here's a HUGE reason why you need email addresses -

Just knowing (and using this) will be worth the price of a high-end marketing course. This is a super powerful tactic -

You can now upload your email list to Facebook, why? Because they can automatically find you more customers just like the ones you already have! Yes, read that again –

Facebook can help you locate more new customers whose profiles match your existing customers. They can do that just by you giving them your current customers' email address.

Think how powerful that is. You can have the power of Facebook's data working for you. If they find a lot of your customers are located in a certain area, like curry, jogging and have 2 kids, they can target ads at other users who match that profile!

You would never be able to get the data on your customers like that. Yet Facebook has it and can find lots of other people just like them and then show them your amazing offer!

Rather than take up lots of book space, this article provides great insight and step-by-step instructions:

http://blog.wishpond.com/post/64215441993/how-to-target-facebook-ads-based-on-email-address

To find out more from Facebook

https://www.facebook.com/business/a/online-sales/lookalike-audiences

I strongly urge you to test it. I have heard some fantastic reports on results people are achieving with it.

Resources

Software I strongly recommend you try:

Mailing List

www.Aweber.com

Squeeze Pages (Highly Recommended)

www.ClickFunnels.com

Others

http://optinmonster.com/ - popups for wordpress
https://www.hellobar.com – signup form
www.unbounce.com – pop up's
http://popupdomination.com/ - pop up's
https://www.optimizely.com/ - split test software
https://vwo.com/ - split test software

Great email marketing blogs

http://blog.mailchimp.com/

http://blog.getresponse.com/

http://blog.aweber.com/

http://www.dotmailer.com/blog/

http://www.emailmonday.com/

Plus you can get even more ideas by joining us FREE at

www.EmailMarketingBonus.com

Thank you

Before you go, I just wanted to say 'thank you' for purchasing this book.

If you're new to email marketing I hope you found it all useful and you are fully inspired to go and create some amazing campaigns that generate amazing results.

If you've already done a lot of email marketing I hope you picked up some new tips / ideas that you can use straight away to increase your results further. Please make sure you have read the 'tip' paragraphs. Just one or two could be worth a fortune.

However whatever you do please take action – unless you take action you are not going to achieve anything! After that, test and improve and watch your results increase. It's amazing what can be done.

Please can I ask you a favour?

If you got one or two tips or ideas from this book that will help you out, please would do me a favour and share your thoughts and let others know?

I would be very grateful if you could please leave a review on Amazon (please just click the link below it will take you straight there)

http://www.Amazon.com

www.ingramcontent.com/pod-product-compliance
Lightning Source LLC
Chambersburg PA
CBHW060632210326
41520CB00010B/1573